TURKEY HUNTING TALES, TIPS AND TACTICS

YOUR GUIDE TO SPRING SUCCESS

JACE BAUSERMAN

CONTENTS

INTRODUCTION

The ice-choked Arkansas rolled gently, its sea-green water spilling over small boulders and pushing effortlessly around sandbars. My dozen mallard fakes swung left and right in the current, eventually earning the attention of a lone drake. He dumped his landing gear and made a quick descent. My Remington 870 thundered and the migrating greenhead hit the snow-covered bank with a thud. A fresh four inches of powdery snow swallowed the bird, but my trusty lab, Ginger, fished him out.

It was late morning when the whistling-wing action came to a halt. I was glad. My fingers were numb and one of my Walmart waders was starting to leak. It had been a good morning—not great but good—and I had two fat mallards and a colorful wood duck to show for my willingness to embrace the frosty temps. Ginger had gotten some good work, and picking up a dozen decoys would take little time.

The water bit my bare fingers and my wet foot burned. Then, unexpectedly, something happened that made me forget all about my discomfort. A flock of wild turkeys streamed out of the snow-cloaked woods in a single-file line.

Their ebony feathers glistened in the December sun. Most had gray heads, but I did pick out a few red domes in the mob. In seconds the feet of the meandering group turned the once-white sandbar brown. They purred and clucked, completely oblivious to my presence. I'd never seen them before, and I'd lived on this river throughout my youth. Finally, as quickly as they appeared, the flock filtered back into the frosted bottom.

I wasn't cold anymore. Now I was awestruck. The walk back to my Ford Ranger was spent replaying the event in mind, trying to figure out where the birds had come from and where they would go. That was the day my fascination with the wild turkey began.

Although I found their tracks in the snow the following day, I never saw the flock again. I wanted to—badly. I made multiple trips in January and February combing the river up and down, but I didn't find any birds.

By late April I'd given up hope of finding them again. Instead, I turned my attention to locating cast deer bone. I had just found the right side of a small 8-point when I heard it. At first I thought my ears were playing tricks on me, but then it rang again, unmistakable this time. It was a gobble. It was a ways off, but it was a gobble. I dropped the shed and ran toward it. I covered 100 yards as fast as my teenaged legs would carry me. I stopped. I couldn't see a thing. I listened. Nothing but wind. Nervous I would never find or hear the spring noisemaker, I took off at full tilt once again. I crashed through the greening-up brush into a clearing. Nothing! I wanted to see him probably more than I'd ever wanted anything in life. Then he sounded off again. He was close. I dropped onto all fours and started crawling down the edge of the opening. I'd gone close to 60 yards and had just slith-ered under a large stand of tamarack when I saw him—a black blob walking up the woodlot toward me. His head was a brilliant color of red, his creamy-tipped tail fan was open and his wing tips scratched the ground. In front of him were three hens. I lay under that tamarack and watched the long-beard court his ladies for over an hour before slithering away undetected.

For the next two years I devoured all the wild turkey literature I could get my hands on. I would lay in bed late at night and read about the springtime adventures of the great turkey writers of the 90s: Jim Casada, Jim Spencer and Brian Lovett, to name a few. After extinguishing my light, I would lay awake, often for hours, dreaming of the day I could match wits with a hard-gobbling longbeard.

At the time, turkey tags in my little corner of Colorado were given on a limited-draw basis. The particular river-bottom unit I planned to hunt allowed only 10 tags each spring. There were some OTC options in the state, but my parents weren't keen on their 16-year-old son driving far from home and camping alone. So, I started applying. As I suspected, the dice came up snake eyes when it came to that spring's turkey draw. The next spring followed suit, and when I got that "Thank you for applying letter ..." in the mail, I was disgusted. I couldn't wait any longer. That July, I applied for a fall turkey tag. Maybe it wouldn't be the sun-soaked gobble barrage I'd dreamed of, but I would be hunting turkeys, and at the end of the day, that was enough.

I scouted every single day for two weeks. I went before school and after. On the weekends, I lived on the river from dawn to dusk. I knew where two small bands of river-bottom Rios were roosting, feeding and killing time in-between. The first group was made up of mostly hens and pullets with a jake or two sprinkled in. The second group was a band of five big toms. They were my focus.

I didn't sleep a wink the night before the opener, and for the first time in my young life, I was the one who woke my father up. He wasn't a hunter, but he knew how much this particular adventure meant to me and wanted to join in. Under the cover of darkness, we inched our way through the timber, being sure to avoid the roost. We set up in a travel corridor the boy band used often.

The birds didn't make a peep on the roost, but shortly after daybreak I heard the unmistakable sound of wing-beats. Then all was quiet. Dad and I sat in silence for over an hour, our eyes dancing back and forth through the timbered bottom. My heart was in my throat the entire time.

I heard them before I saw them—the sound of crispy cottonwood leaves being tossed recklessly about tipped me off. The birds were scratching for seeds and insects and heading in our direction. I lifted my Remington 870 and rested it on my already shaking knee. I tried to control my breathing, but it was impossible. When the first bird came into view I could hardly get my index finger to manipulate my safety. It was just a hen, but on that day and at that exact moment in time, it might as well have been a gobbler sporting two-inch spurs.

She scratched around a while before a few other hens joined her. Then the entire group started walking right toward us. I could hear my dad breathing hard. I was trembling. I slammed the trigger. That's the one thing I do remember about the exact moment I fired at my first wild turkey. By the grace of God, my load of lead #6's crushed the bird's head and neck. My dad hugged me. No, it was more than that—he practically squeezed the life out of me and I loved every minute of it. It was a great moment, and one I will cherish for the rest of my days.

Since that first fall hen, my love affair with the wild

turkey has only become more intense. I simply can't get enough of them, and though I still tote a shotgun into the woods from time to time, my fascination with the stick and string means I run more arrows through wing butts than #6's through red heads these days.

I wrote this book with one goal in mind: to help you, the archery turkey hunter. No one gave me a dime to put it out, and the tips and tactics to come are from years of in-the-woods experience. Apply them, and you will be successful. As for the gear, it's the gear I trust and use. So, kick back in the recliner and let's dive into the exciting world of archery turkey hunting.

DEDICATION

This book is dedicated to my lovely bride, Amy, and my three amazing children: Hunter, Abbey and Brody.

Romans 3:23-24—For all have sinned and fall short of the glory of God, and all are justified freely by his grace through the redemption that came by Christ Jesus.

MOUNTAIN MERRIAM'S

The crafty Merriam's inhabits the mountainous and canyon regions of the western United States. Originally introduced into the ponderosa pine forests of Colorado, Arizona and New Mexico, the birds have since been transplanted into Utah, Idaho, Washington, Oregon, California, Montana, Wyoming, Nebraska and South Dakota. In some states, like Colorado, Nebraska and South Dakota, Merriam's gobblers have bred with Rio Grande hens. The result is a bird that doesn't boast the snow-white fan Merriam's hunters crave.

Currently, the Merriam's population is estimated at around 335,000, and according to the National Wild Turkey Federation (www.nwtf.org), the Rocky Mountains are considered the central hub for harvesting a pure Merriam's bird.

Nomadic, opportunistic feeders, Merriam's birds will wander to high altitudes during the spring and summer, following the snow line. The area just below the snow line boasts the newest, freshest shoots of plant life, as well as emerging bug life. It's not uncommon for birds to wander above 10,000 feet. During the winter months, when snow comes to the high country, birds will wander into the foothills where they will spend the winter in large flocks. These birds are great travelers, and depending on factors such as weather, food and predation, they can travel more than 40 miles.

Merriam's gobblers are as black as the ace of spades with blue, purple and bronze reflections that are only distinguishable through a quality pair of optics or when gazing on a downed bird. A mature tom will typically mirror the size of a large Eastern bird, and many experts disagree on which subspecies is the largest. Merriam's toms will tip the scales at 18 to 30 pounds, with most falling in the middle part of that range. Females are naturally smaller and boast buff-tipped breast feathers that are not nearly as dark as those of male birds.

In terms of sheer volume, Merriam's birds have the weakest gobble of the four subspecies, and due to the rocky terrain they call home, they sport shorter, more spindly beards. Because their spurs often rub on rocks and other rough debris, they're also typically much shorter.

So what does it take to walk out of the woods with a whiter-than-snow fan bobbing over your shoulder?

If you've hunted turkeys for any amount of time, you've likely heard someone say, "Merriam's are dumb birds. They gobble at anything and come running to calls." Here's my response to this statement: bull crap! The truth is, hunters who say things like that are usually chasing unpressured birds on strictly managed ground. Of course those turkeys going to be a little dumb. But in most real-world hunting situations, Merriam's can be as crafty as any of the other three subspecies found in the U.S.

Like all turkey subspecies, Merriam's boast incredible

eyesight. Due to the fact that these birds have large home ranges, they are very difficult to put a pin on.

Years ago, I pedaled deep (13 miles) into a remote pinyon- and cedar-lined canyon in search of a public-land Merriam's gobbler. The Colorado season was only two days away, and I wanted to get a jump on the competition. Later that evening, while perched on a large rock, I detected twelve different toms and a pile of hens meandering down the river toward some large cottonwoods. I put the birds to bed and quietly slipped out of the area.

NOTE: Do me a favor and don't ever fall into the "I'm not gonna work that hard for a turkey" crowd. I'm not saying you have to mountain bike 13 miles, but if you want to consistently kill birds, especially birds on public or highly pressured private land, you're going to have to put out a little extra effort and often think outside the box.

I RETURNED with a good friend on opening morning. We'd left the trailhead at 2 a.m., and by the time our Double Bull blind was set in a large sage flat the birds were using as a strut zone, the glow of the eastern sun was beginning to tease the canyon to life. To my excitement, the leafless cottonwoods were filled with black blobs, and a symphony of springtime gobbles rang out. Two hours later, my hunting partner skewered a large tom, and I skipped an arrow under the breast of a bird less than three yards away. Yep, I had a turkey meltdown. It happens.

We remained in the blind, letting my thoroughly confused tom melt into the tamarack brush. Through my binos, I kept tabs on the other ten toms and hens—toms and hens that had long passed out of bow range before a pair of lovesick two-year-olds showed up on the scene. They kept going ... and going ... and going. It was like watching an Energizer Bunny commercial. In fact, the group never stopped. I know, because I've ridden the canyon many times, and from the position we were in, I could see at least three miles back to the east. The meandering birds covered that distance in no time.

We hoped the mob would return that evening, but we were skeptical at the same time. We decided to set up along the river between a pair of roost sites (one being the roost the birds had used that morning). Guess what? Not one bird returned to that roost. Fortunately, a pair of boisterous gobblers wandered into our decoy spread from the opposite direction the morning birds had gone. At 20 yards, my arrow was true, and my hunting partner and I capped off a Colorado public-land double.

I hope that helps you understand just how nomadic Merriam's birds are. These turkeys had used and returned to the same roost for at least three days that I knew of. Then, for whatever reason, they decided to pitch down one morning, walk miles away and not return. Yes, I know pressure moves animals like nothing else, but we were the only ones at the trailhead that morning, and all but two of those birds had long passed our position before we launched arrows.

Weeks later I returned to the area with another hunting buddy who'd yet to punch his tag. The turkey rut had progressed and the early-spring flocks had dissipated. We hunted hard for two days and were able to put eyes on only two different toms.

As far as Merriam's birds being easy to call, I've found them no easier to bring within shotgun or bow range than any of the other three subspecies. As with calling any bird, the period of the rut, hunting pressure, weather and other factors all play a role in how responsive a bird will be to sexy hen talk.

What I have found to be true is that Merriam's birds seem more willing to close large distances in response to calls. Does that make them stupid? No! Due to the vastness of the landscape these birds often call home, it's not uncommon for a walk-about tom to respond and come to a live-hen call that barely tickles his eardrums.

When calling Merriam's birds, I prefer to run calls that carry great distances and cut the all-to-often howling western wind. My favorite reach-out-and-touch-their-ears Merriam's call is a trusty box call. Box calls get a bad rap. When I give seminars, I hear a lot of negative comments about them. They're too easy to use. Every hunter on the planet hammers away on them. They don't work on public land. You can't get the exact pitch you want. I could go on forever with the complaints I've heard from hunters about box calls.

Here's my opinion on the matter. They work great to cut the western winds. They also work great when trying to raise the interest of a distant tom. On multiple occasions, I've been able to sit behind a quality spotting scope and watch a tom 500 yards away take notice of my box call. Once you master them, box calls can produce pitch-perfect tones. I especially feel this is the case when using a true chalk-on-wood system.

Another Merriam's eardrum ringer is an aluminum pot-and-peg call. I've found aluminum pot calls carry great distances. I'm also a fan of glass. What I love about pot-and-peg calls is that I can easily adjust the volume and pitch simply by swapping strikers. And that's not all. Once you really know what you're doing, these calls produce, in my opinion, simply the best turkey tones.

Like many turkey fanatics, my go-to call is a diaphragm. Through this wonderful industry I've been blessed to hunt with two NWTF Grand National Calling Champions—Billy Yargus and Josh Grossenbacher—and I learned a lot from both of these wonderful gentlemen. Yes, I work in the outdoor industry, but as I mentioned in the introduction, no one paid me a dime to put this book out, and I can promise you that Josh's Zink Signature Series calls (www.zinkcalls.com) and Billy's M.A.D. Billy Yargus calls (www.flambeauoutdoors.com) are some of the best I've ever used. I'm also a big fan of Rocky Mountain Hunting Calls. Though this brand is better known in the elk world, Rocky Jacobson and his team also love to chase longbeards, and their mouth calls are some of favorites.

Regardless of which one you choose, the key to any diaphragm is practice, practice and more practice. I highly recommend buying a bunch of mouth calls in the off-season and wearing out the reeds before turkey season. My favorite method when for mastering a diaphragm is to listen to live turkey sounds. I record these sounds when I'm in the woods, but you can also find them on YouTube. You can listen to great callers like Yargus and Grossenbacher on YouTube as well.

Once I feel like I'm starting to sound like a turkey, I record myself and then match my sounds against the recorded calls. While mine will never be as good, it sure gives me a great scale to match up against. In addition, I practice a lot in the car, while cleaning the garage and when performing other mundane tasks. It's also a good idea to call in front of friends and family. I've been around a lot of hunters—both turkey and elk—that are great at calling when no one is around but choke in the heat of the moment.

Two years ago, while chasing Merriam's at around 9,000 feet in the public mountains of Colorado, I encountered a pair of wonderful gentleman. I was toting a bow, they were toting shotguns. It was mid-May and the birds had been heavily pressured. After visiting with my newfound friends for a few minutes it became clear the only calls in their vests were diaphragm calls. Unfortunately, all but the two calls they were using were still in their packages, and the hunters told me they'd only opened and started using their selected calls hours earlier. Yikes!

Without a blind and hunting heavily pressured birds on public land, I knew I was mostly spinning my wheels, so I offered to sit and call for them. They were only too happy to accept my invitation.

I located a meadow alive with bug life. The grass wasn't too tall (turkeys generally don't like grasses, especially wet grasses, that come up too high on them), and after locating a few feathers and droppings, we decided the spot was as good as any.

Knowing the birds had been pressured for weeks, I called very little, never cutting or yelping. Instead, I used soft, subtle yelps and a few purrs. To this day I'm not sure if the lone longbeard wandered into the meadow to appease his rumbling gut or to investigate my calling. Regardless of the reason, he came in on a string once entering the meadow. My calling didn't alarm him or put him on alert, and moments later one of the gentlemen put a load of Federal #5's into his cranium.

Another thing I've found to be true when chasing the white-tipped Merriam's is this: the deeper you go, the better your experience will be. The West is big, right? Most public land and national forest areas are measured in square miles rather than acres. You can get away from the crowds, especially since many turkey hunters aren't willing to put a great deal of effort into bagging a bird. How do I know? I experience this season after season. In fact, a few years back, I startled a couple of gentlemen sleeping in their tents at a particular Colorado trailhead. This area is known for a robust Merriam's population, and thus it attracts a fair number of hunters.

It was 3 a.m. when I heard them rustling around in their tent. I was loading down my pack and preparing for the long walk in. Seconds before I started down the trail, the duo emerged. One joked, "What are you gonna do, shoot one out of the roost?" His partner laughed. I simply smiled and told them the name of the canyon I was planning to get to. The jokester looked me dead in the eye and said, "If that's what I have to do to kill a turkey, I don't want to kill one. That's a miserable hike. And if you do kill one, you have to pack it back out." I didn't respond. I simply shook their hands and went on my way.

Three hours later I found myself not knowing which direction to go. Birds were gobbling to my north, south, east and west. It was insane—the type of morning you dream about. Because I wasn't toting a blind, I decided to stay put and hollow out the bottom of a big cedar. My makeshift blind was ready in minutes, and I placed my decoys. (For decoys, I typically tote realistic inflatable Avian-X fakes into the backcountry.) The entire time, of course, birds were gobbling like crazy.

I grabbed my slate and let out a few soft yelps. The birds thundered back. I matched their intensity and started to yelp and cut. Each time I cut, the birds only gobbled harder, their booming voices reverberating off the canyon walls. It wasn't a matter of if birds were going to come—it was a matter of how many would arrive and from which direction.

It was the birds to the west—three toms followed by a gaggle of jakes—that scrambled into view first. The birds were so entranced with the decoys and with each other that they never saw me draw my bow. I picked out the biggest tom in the bunch and splashed a Rage-powered Easton arrow through his lungs.

After removing the innards and strapping the bird to my pack, I started the long march back to my Chevy. On the way, I passed fourteen other hunters, all toting shotguns. I spoke to several, and it seemed that the success rates closer to the trailhead were dismal.

When I arrived back at my truck, the gentlemen I visited with earlier that morning were cooking up lunch. "It's a damn madhouse down there," said the vocal one. "This is just ridiculous. Guys were running birds off the roost. I mean, it wasn't even safe."

They hadn't noticed the bird strapped to my pack, but when they did, that's when things really got interesting. The quieter one said, "Wow, what a beautiful bird. That is just awesome. If I can have a chance at a bird like that and keep away from people, I'm willing to go." His partner snorted at him, but he followed me to my truck, and I showed him the exact flocculation of my successful hunt on the map. I'm not sure if the two ever ventured into that canyon or not, but I like to think they did.

When it comes to western birds on public land, don't be afraid to burn some boot leather. Separate yourself from the masses and find those pockets of hidden birds—birds that are often more than willing to come to sexy hen talk and a quality decoy spread.

2

RIDICULOUS RIOS

Of the forty-nine states that allow turkey hunting, fourteen of them offer the Rio Grande subspecies. Texas, due to its massive size, management model and ideal habitat, leads the charge when it comes to overall population of these birds. Other notable Rio states include Kansas, Oklahoma, Nebraska (you will find some hybrids) and South Dakota. Nationwide, the population of the Rio subspecies is well over one million birds strong.

Named after the famous Rio Grande River, the Rio Grande subspecies, like the Merriam's, is a nomadic, opportunistic feeder. Multiple studies have shown Rios will wander more than ten miles from their winter feeding grounds to their spring breeding grounds. Highly adaptable to an array of climates, the Rio often prefers to roost in the tallest tree it can find, and if that tree happens to be along a brush-choked waterway, all the better. While Rios can and do thrive in a number of pine forests, the bird prefers mesquite, scrub oak, and basically any brush along a creek or river system.

Not nearly as dark as its Merriam's cousin, the Rio has longer legs, and its most distinguishing color is a coppery hue. The tail fan showcases yellowish-tan tips that are much lighter than the Osceola or Eastern but darker than the Merriam's. On average, hens tip the scales between 8 and 13 pounds, and a mature tom will have a fighting weight around 20 pounds.

I've successfully hunted Rios in Colorado, Kansas, Nebraska, Oklahoma and Texas, and the key ingredient to being a Rio killer is having a solid pre-hunt plan. Rios are creatures of habit, and if left undisturbed, they will often hit the same roost and strutting areas day after day. Do your homework ahead of time, locate the birds, note their travel patterns and make a game plan.

It's my opinion that Rios are the most vocal of all the turkey subspecies, which makes calling to these birds an absolute riot. As for decoys, the more realistic the better, and I typically run a Dave Smith's Breeding Pair (a DSD ¾ Strut Jake and Submissive Hen) and place a feeding hen off to the side. Just make sure that when you set up the Breeding Pair that you leave room between the jake and the hen for an approaching tom to walk between. I've found toms like to walk between the jake and hen in an effort to show dominance and go face to face with the jake.

In the spring of 2017, I arrived for a DIY Rio hunt on a buddy's ranch in Texas. The ranch had never been hunted for birds, and this was to be my friend's inaugural spring turkey adventure. Unfortunately, two months prior to our hunt, a severe wildfire ripped through the ranch and left it charred. Only a few roost trees remained, and, thanks to the new growth and thriving bug life, birds were numerous. While that was certainly good, the ranch lacked adequate cover. We could easily glass and spot birds from long distances, but they could spot us as well.

I arrived at the ranch with plenty of daylight left to hunt, but I opted to heed the advice given at the beginning of this chapter and do my homework first. I spent the afternoon and evening hours driving ranch roads, gaining vantage points and glassing. Due to regular ranch and oil-truck traffic, the birds tolerated a vehicle with four wheels better than a two-legged figure roaming about.

With the light waning, I located three birds moving toward a trio of large cottonwoods at the base of a small pond. I left the truck, climbed a hill and set up my spotting scope. Two gobblers were tailing a hen, and upon reaching a small hill adjacent to the trees, they flew up for the evening.

Having never been to the area before, I snapped some pictures of the landscape on my iPhone, pulled up an aerial map of the area using my onX Hunt App and dropped a pin on the location I planned to put my blind.

Knowing how open the landscape was, I toted my decoys, blind and other gear into the area well before the break of day. I wanted to set up in total darkness and knew even a small sliver of light would tip my hand. Using my phone and the pin I dropped on its mapping system, I made my way to the area I'd found the evening before. Under the cover of darkness, I was able to set up my blind and decoys without ever alerting the birds.

NOTE: I was careful not to press too close to the roost. I see lots of hunters do this and it's just a bad idea, even if you go in super early. Like all game animals, the life of a turkey revolves around survival. They are under constant threat from coyotes, bobcats and other predators, and they don't miss much when it comes to something pressing in on their sleeping grounds. Trust your calling and your decoys. Set up off the roost (I like to be 150 to 200 yards away) and let the birds work to you.

As LIGHT BROKE, the pair of toms got extremely vocal. They would face the hen and gobble their heads off. The hen actually turned away from the toms and never showed a bit of interest. She didn't let out so much as a church-mouse-quiet tree yelp. The toms were excited, and though I don't typically call much until birds get on the ground—other than a few soft tree yelps—I opted to get pretty vocal.

NOTE: I get asked a lot about calling. How much to call, what calls to use, etc. Here's the deal. Listen more and call less. I let the birds I'm hunting tell me how and when to call based on how much they're talking and, if I can see them, their body language. This also helps me know just how aggressive to be.

WATCHING the birds through my binos, I noticed they did an about-face the second I let out a series of yelps. As soon as they saw my decoys, the duo got even more boisterous. As light continued to fill the landscape, I continued to match the intensity of the birds. I wanted to let them know that there was a willing hen nearby and remind them that the lady they had in close quarters was ignoring them. It worked. Then hen exited the roost headed in one direction, and the pair of two-year-olds headed another.

It was obvious they were locked on to the DSDs, and

there was no reason to call again. The birds came in quickly and started abusing my jake decoy badly. I shot one of them. The second I did, the other tom jumped on top the jake, giving me plenty of time to load a second arrow and dump the bird while he dug his spurs into the imposter decoy. It was awesome.

NOTE: When bowhunting turkeys from a blind, always have a few arrows (I prefer three) out of your quiver. The purpose is twofold. First, today's bows are so quiet that, should you whiff, oftentimes the bird or birds will be so entranced with the decoy setup they will offer you another shot. Having to dig around in your quiver with your heart in your throat while trying to keep an eye on the bird or birds takes time, creates movement and can be noisy. Having a few arrows resting against the blind allows for a quick follow-up shot. Secondly, as was the case with this hunt, a second bird may be so fired up and so irritated with the jake imposter that he pays no mind to the fate of his buddy. As I have many times before, I was able to pull off a double.

NOTE: I believe if there is one piece of equipment turkey hunters overlook, it's optics. Optics play a huge role in turkey hunting. They are pivotal for scouting, and I like to use them to watch birds from my ground blind. Countless times I've spotted lone toms slipping in silently, and in this case, I was able to keep an eye on the body language of the birds in the trees. I could see them face my position and gobble, which told me a lot about just how aggressive I should get with my calling.

3

EGOTISTICAL EASTERNS

I love Eastern birds. Better yet, I love hunting Eastern birds in big timber. There gobbles boom and echo, and for me, there simply isn't another subspecies quite like them.

I've hunted Eastern birds in Kansas, Missouri, Oklahoma and Louisiana. If you've spent enough time discussing turkeys with other hunters, you've likely heard that Eastern birds are generally pretty skittish and difficult to call. Here's what I've discovered: heavily pressured Eastern gobblers can be ghosts and are super difficult to call bowhunting-close. Eastern birds on lightly pressured public or private ground are as killable as any other subspecies.

What makes Eastern birds so dang hard? Two things: pressure and terrain. There are simply more licensed turkey hunters east of the Mississippi, and more hunters means more pressure. As for the terrain, Eastern turkey habit can be thick and swampy, boasting everything from long ridges to deep hollows to miles of rolling hardwoods. Birds can simply get lost and never be found.

As far as top Eastern states, Missouri and Iowa consistently produce birds that break the 25-pound mark, and both offer a good amount of public land. Other great Eastern states include Arkansas, Louisiana, Georgia, Illinois, North Carolina and Tennessee. Just know that this list represents a small percentage of the states that harbor Eastern birds. Eastern turkeys are, by current counts, the most populous of all subspecies. In fact, Easterns outnumber all other subspecies combined. Recent population counts put the current population of Eastern birds well north of 5.3 million. In all, the Eastern bird inhabits 38 states and several Canadian provinces.

A mature Eastern tom will average 4 feet high and can weigh up to 30 pounds. Toms sport chestnut-brown tips and tail feathers and white and black bars on the wings. Females typically weight between 8 and 12 pounds. Eastern birds have the strongest gobble of all subspecies, and their beards are also the longest.

When it comes to the groceries Eastern birds crave, the list is long. This is due to the variety of landscapes these highly adaptable birds inhabit. Eastern birds enjoy a diet of insects, grains, grasses and fruits.

My first archery Eastern adventure took place in Kansas. Though the state is home to a healthy Rio population, I was hunting in the eastern half near Topeka. The land I was hunting was private, but it received a fair amount of pressure throughout the year. Numerous individuals had permission to hunt it, and at the time of my trip, shotgun season was in full swing.

After visiting with a local friend and getting a tour of the property, I did some low-impact scouting and put some birds to bed. The birds took shelter in a large stand of hardwoods, and the first open area near their roost was a small grassy valley located more than 300 yards away. The valley was rich with bugs and filled with tender shoots of green. The next day, I went in early and deployed my blind.

It was a gorgeous morning. The wind was calm and the cool spring air bit at my nose. With the first ray of sunlight came a gobble. Another echoed back, this one down the draw and deeper in the timber. Another followed it, and then another. It was shaping up to be an epic morning, and I knew it was just a matter of time before a few birds wandered into my little clearing.

I was right. A pair of energetic gobblers—two-year-olds seeing who could out-gobble the other—popped into the clearing about 80 yards away. They spotted my hen and jake combo instantly, blew up into strut and started coming. I was certain my first Sunflower State tag was as good as punched. Then something happened. Both birds, as if on cue, deflated, stretched their necks, putted and dashed off.

After the birds cleared the opening, I hopped out of the blind and scrutinized my decoys. All was good. I looked at my blind, and although it wasn't brushed in, it looked fine. I did have it backed up to some heavy pines, but I'd taken no extra lengths to blend it in. I checked my windows; nothing wrong there. Scratching my head, I climbed back into the blind.

A few minutes passed and the woods got quiet. The nonstop, hammering-on-the roost gobbling had subsided, so I decided to let out a few soft yelps. The response was immediate. A lone tom sounded off. He was close, and just as I was getting ready to touch striker to slate, he popped into the clearing. Then, just like that, he was gone. The tom took one look at my setup, putted and dashed away. I was furious. Sadly, this scenario played out two more times before I decided to pack up and call it a morning.

The evening hunt was uneventful. I decided to back out

of the meadow, and actually headed to another property miles away. I'd already spooked five gobblers, and I wanted to let things cool down a little. My evening property was full of birds, and though I got a few toms to answer me, I wasn't able to lay eyes on a single live bird.

I spent the night thinking about my morning mishaps and what I was going to do differently. I came to the conclusion that the birds had been pressured more than I'd previously thought, and I decided to go without any decoys. I was going to set up in a slightly different spot in the meadow and see if I could get a bird to simply wander by.

Not having any decoys, I decided to leave the calls in my vest and just let the morning unfold. Like the previous morning, the birds hammered on the roost, and twenty minutes after fly-down, I had three toms and nine hens in the meadow. Unfortunately, the second the birds started to work in my direction they putted and ran like they'd been shot at. Disgusted, I jumped out of my Double Bull, broke it down, and hollowed out a hole in a big evergreen. It was obvious now that the not-brushed-in-blind was the problem.

As I was erecting my natural fort, three jakes waddled in and busted me. This only fueled my fire. Have I mentioned how much I love to shoot jakes? Realizing my ground blind had been the problem, I slipped back to my truck and grabbed my decoys, set them out and climbed into my newly constructed hide. Two hours later, after going back and forth with a reluctant-to-commit tom, I was finally able to get my bow back and hammer the bruiser as he Jean-Claude Van Dammed my jake decoy.

With a tag left in my pocket and one morning left to hunt, I spent the remainder of the day brushing in my ground blind. When I was done, it had disappeared in a quagmire of snipped evergreen branches. I'd never before gone to that length of blind disguise when bowhunting wild turkeys.

The meadow was a hot zone, and I pray I will be able to hunt that fabulous property again one day. Given that I'd put so much pressure on the meadow for two mornings in a row, I wondered how the hunt would be on the third morning. Honestly, I had my doubts about the wisdom of trying again, but those doubts quickly faded when a quintet of gobbling longbeards strutted into the meadow. I called. The birds took one look at the decoys, and it was a flat-out race to see who could get there first. Looking back, I honestly believe I could have killed all three of those gobblers. After shooting the largest bird in the group, a mature tom that ended up weighing 27.1 pounds, I watched the other two birds as they stayed in the spread for over an hour. They were infatuated with the decoys and were in full-on rut mode.

NOTE: Up until my Eastern experience, I never put much thought into my blind setup. Of course, I always gave a good deal of thought as to where I would set it, but I never really made it disappear. I always tried to set it up against cover, but honestly, I've killed birds in wide-open wheat fields more than once. However, when I hunt Easterns now, I always, always, always go to great lengths to brush in my blind. My good buddy, outdoor writer and stone-cold turkey killer Tony Peterson, told me that when it comes to being comfortable with blinds, Eastern birds are simply different. "They just don't tolerate [blinds] the way other birds will," he said. "Most of my turkey experience has come hunting pressured Minnesota birds, and I'm often amazed at how well they can pick out a ground blind."

NOTE:

If you're going to be a turkey killer, especially with archery tackle, you better be willing to be flexible. You can't get stuck in a rut. You must be willing to step outside the norm and figure out what's going on. Take this hunt for example. I could've stayed in my blind, but I knew something was bugging the birds. After seeing them run away at Mach 10 with no decoys in the meadow, I knew they were picking out the blind. This was their area, and they were very aware any changes. Rather than calling it a morning, I got creative and built a natural hide.

4

ONLY THE OSCEOLA

This will be the shortest chapter in this book. Why? Because I don't want to fill you with knowledge I don't have. I write to teach, help and educate, and when it comes to the wily Osceola, I simply haven't spent enough time hunting them. However, don't turn the page. I do have some experience hunting the Osceola, and, oh, what a hunt it was.

The Osceola has made Florida a hot spot for turkey fanatics. This is the only state in the country—and the only location in the world—where hunters can kill an Osceola bird and complete their Wild Turkey Grand Slam.

NOTE: If you head to Florida with hopes of tagging an Osceola, you need to pay attention to where in the state you are. Florida has a robust Eastern population as well, and if you don't pay attention to your geography, your hopes of a Grand Slam could be dashed in a hurry. According to the NWTF, Osceola gobblers inhabit central Florida as well as the southern part of the state. Northern Florida is Eastern country, and though you may stumble across a few hybrids, they will not be pure Osceola birds. For specific information on the actual Eastern/Osceola line, I highly encourage you to visit the NWTF's subspecies map.

NOTE: Florida has plenty of public land, but it gets hammered for birds. Unless you have access to an airboat, which many serious Floridian turkey fanatics do, you may find yourself elbow to elbow with other hunters. Though it is pricy, I highly recommend going with a reputable outfitter. An outfitter will have access to private land, and they will know what the birds in the area are doing. Osceolas can be tough customers, and a good outfitter is worth his/her weight in gold. Plus, if you've done your homework and use a reputable outfitter, you'll know you're hunting actual Osceola birds. Another option if you're looking to pull off an Osceola hunt is to do a little social media surfing and see if you can't arrange a hunt swap. There are plenty of Florida turkey hunters with access to private land dying to shoot a Merriam's or Rio Grande.

ALSO KNOWN as the Florida turkey, the Osceola features white bars on the wings that are much narrower and feature a more irregular, broken pattern than other subspecies. In addition, the slim white bars of the Osceola don't extend to the feather shaft. Feathers with dark-brown tips make up the tail fan, and adult males typically bounce right around the 20-pound mark. Females weigh between 8 and 12 pounds. The Osceola has long legs, longer spurs than most subspecies and thick, sizable beards.

Osceolas thrive in the swamps, palmettos and cattle

pastures of southern Florida. The deep swamps and marshes allow the birds to escape hunting pressure. The birds will roost in big oaks, stands of flat pines and even cypress trees. As for grub, these Sunshine State birds will eat small reptiles like lizards and snakes, but they prefer a craw full of beechnuts, acorns and grasses.

Many consider the Osceola to be the most difficult bird to call in, and stories of their unwillingness to gobble spread far and wide. Maybe I just got lucky, but my one-day Osceola hunt with Hoppy Kempfer at Osceola Outfitters (www.osceolaoutfitters.com) was anything but quiet.

It was the last day of the 2017 season, and with only one day to hunt, Hoppy and I weren't overly optimistic about our chances. Though Hoppy has thousands of acres of prime Osceola dirt, he had run several hunters through his camp, and given that it was late in the rut, we figured finding a tom willing to commit was going to be pretty difficult.

Hoppy had pulled all of his blinds down, and he wasn't a fan of us popping one up and hoping the birds wouldn't notice. He explained to me that the birds were incredibly wary and noted that us tossing out a ground blind would spook them. I really wanted to attempt to harvest one with my bow, so Hoppy decided a natural ground blind would be best.

Though we were by no means inundated with gobbles, we had plenty of distant tom talk to keep us interested. Hoppy is one of the best callers I've ever hunted with—he calls only with his mouth and doesn't use a diaphragm— and he had multiple gobblers going back and forth.

Our morning hide was inside a large stand of palmettos. Hoppy and I, along with our mutual friend Mark Sidelinger, spent some time cutting palm branches and building an elaborate blind. While we were working, Hoppy explained that the Osceola, much like the Eastern, often won't tolerate a pop-up-style blind that hasn't been out for a long period of time, and that the natural look was going to be better than trying to blend one in.

Fog from the heavy humidity lifted in the cattle pastures as the sun rose. It was a beautiful sight, and there is truly nothing quite like being smack in the middle of an ancient Florida swamp. The sights, sounds and smells are something every turkey hunter should experience at least once.

An hour passed, and the gobbling activity had ceased. Then, I caught a glimpse of a red head bobbing through the palmettos. The bird wasn't in strut, and when he reached the decoy spread he would only stick his head out from behind the cover. Not once did he expose his vitals, and before I could get rid of my bow and pick up the 20-gauge Hoppy had propped against a nearby palmetto, the bird turned and vanished into the thick vegetation. I was sick.

An hour later, for one reason or another, I turned to whisper something to Hoppy and saw a lone tom moving down the two-track to the south. He had no idea we were in the neighborhood, but by the time I was able to pick up the Benelli and settle my bead, the bird was gone.

"Dang it!" Hoppy exclaimed. "You just don't get many chances with these birds. I think we're basically done here. We can try one place on the way out, but it's gonna be run-and-gun, and you'll need to leave that bow in the truck."

Knowing my Grand Slam hopes were fading and that there was only hours left in the season, I agreed.

"There is a deep swamp back here," Hoppy said, pointing into the distance. "Between us and the swamp is a little strip of dry ground the birds like to use. Let's crawl up this hill and put our glasses to work."

Hoppy hit the hill first, and by the time I started my

crawl, he was holding his binos to his eyes with one hand and giving me a thumbs up with the other. My heart leapt in my throat and I slowly slithered up the small embankment. When I reached the top, Hoppy whispered, "Just to the left of that big tree is a tom feeding." Looking closer, I spied the bird as he stabbed his beak into the ground, picking up some midmorning goodies.

The bird was about 100 yards away and was working to our left, but the second Hoppy called, he turned on a dime. He wasn't coming hard, but he was coming. The yardage melted away, and before long the bird was standing in a small opening 30 yards in front of us. "Kill him now," Hoppy instructed. I didn't hesitate, and my load of #5's found its mark. I was thrilled. In fact, I jumped up on the crest of the hill and then took off running down the opposite side. I wanted to see my bird. Touch him. Hold him. My Grand Slam was complete.

When Hoppy got to me, he grabbed the bird's feet, inspected the spurs and said, "You lucky son of a gun. I swear you have a lucky horseshoe up your butt." I've hunted with Hoppy before for hogs, deer and gators and have killed some true brutes. The bird sported a thick, 10 ½-inch beard and almost 2-inch spurs that hooked at the end. A true limb-hanger for sure.

NOTE: Remember, you may be down, but you're never out. During my time in the turkey woods, I've killed a pile of birds on the last day of a hunt. Granted, I only had a day to hunt in Florida, but despite coming close twice and honestly feeling like the hunt was over, we just kept going. If you hope to find consistent success, you need to be relentless in the field.

5

FOUL-WEATHER BIRDS

A s turkey hunters, we live for sun-soaked windless days. The problem is we get so few of them. After spending a few hours sifting through the last five years of turkey hunts in my journal, I found I had only fourteen of what I described as picture-perfect turkey days. My total days spent in the field chasing birds during this five-year stint was sixty-four.

During the course of a spring, I've hunted in hurricane-like winds, sub-zero temps, blizzards, hail and monsoon rains. No, these conditions aren't ideal. In fact, sometimes they flat-out suck. However, if there is one thing I want you to glean from this book, it's this: turkeys will still be out there being turkeys. They're still going to fly off the roost, they're still going to feed and, if a tom is given the chance, he's still going to ... well, you know. If you can embrace difficult weather, your success rate will soar. And often, for public-land hunters and those with access to pressured private ground, you will have the turkey woods all to yourself. Yes, you will likely have to adjust your tactics and may not experience the gobbling action we all crave, but you will likely get into birds.

Here are three foul-weather examples and how my hunting partners and I found success on each.

A KANSAS MONSOON

My two hunting partners and I questioned our own sanity when we woke up to nearly 1.5 inches of rain and a Kansas thunderstorm that continued to drive water down from the heavens. But with only three days to hunt and knowing the land we had permission on was frequented by other hunters, we had to give it go.

Our windshield wipers couldn't keep up with the driving rain, and the already-slippery dirt roads got muddier by the second. We didn't want to carve huge trenches in the landowner's roads, so we parked on the side of the road and made the long, wet and very muddy walk in.

NOTE: Gaining permission to hunt private land is getting harder and harder. If and when you score permission, you must protect the land like it's one of your own children. Part of keeping permission is simply being smart. Treat the land you're hunting well, and you may find yourself with access to a slice of turkey heaven for years and years to come. One stupid lapse in judgment is a quick way to get booted.

THE GLOPPY MUD clung to our rubber boots, and our rain gear was no match for the driving sheets of rain. By the time we got our Double Bull deployed in the underwater winter wheat field, the three of us were soaked to the bone and watching lightning in the distance. The water in the field was actually running. It came in under the blind, carving a little ditch. It was the worst rain I'd ever experienced.

Honestly, we would have left. The lightning wasn't safe, and by no means am I recommending hunting in it, but we were young and thought we were invincible. It also helped that our smartphones told us the lightning was three miles away and moving away from our current position. Mostly, though, only one thing kept us glued to our seats peering out the blind windows, and that was the gobbles that would follow each blast of thunder.

A short time later my buddy Grafton spied the birds. He could count at least eight, and he could see two of the birds stretch their necks and gobble when the thunder rolled. The flock was roosted right on the edge of the field. With the wind and rain we knew they would be reluctant to fly down in the timber, and we grew increasingly optimistic about our rainy-day turkey plan.

NOTE: Rainy day birds are often very visible. Typically, especially when the rain is accompanied by wind, birds prefer open fields, meadows and clearings in the timber. Rain and wind create noise and movement in the timber. The noise of battering rain mixed with swaying branches makes detecting an approaching predator hard. Also, wet feathers mean birds will need a few extra steps before taking flight, and this is much easier accomplished in a large opening than in heavy timber.

MINUTES after the birds pitched down, I sent a few yelps in their direction. They didn't respond, but the two toms and three jakes did give a look in our direction and immediately started walking. They group was 350 yards away, and I never called again. There was no reason to. They never deviated course and, though they made no noise, they never broke stride. When the pair of gobblers and trio of jakes were 50 yards out, they all broke into a flat run, which was comical to watch in the slippery conditions. Even funnier was the fact that the pair of toms tried to blow up into strut in front of our jake decoy but actually couldn't due to their soaked feathers. I was up first, and as was typically the case early in my archery turkey career, I shot under one of the toms. Oblivious to my error, the birds stayed right in the decoys. Grafton, who was up next, simply handed me another arrow and said, "Take your time." Our other buddy, Josh, was trying to run video and keep a very expensive camera dry. My second arrow was true, and the fatally wounded bird collapsed where the field met the timber.

Although the second tom followed his buddy to the field edge, the jakes stayed in the spread. Grafton took advantage of the situation and pounded a stubby-bearded jake. Needless to say, we weren't wet and cold any longer, and the long, heavy haul back to the truck was sweet.

Missouri **Downpour**

It had been a grind in the Show Me State. I'd logged over 20 hours in a blind in hopes of bringing a willing tom into bow range. I'd made setup after setup, but at the end of two full days, I had nothing to show for my efforts.

That evening, over a warm dinner, I struck up a conversation with renowned turkey hunter and champion turkey caller Billy Yargus.

"The weather looks bad tomorrow," Billy told me.

"Gonna be tough to get a bird fired up, but I'm planning to go. I would be happy to take you and try to call you in a rainy-day bird, but I have one stipulation, and that is you leave that bow at home and take my 12-gauge."

Billy wasn't much for the stick and string when it came to longbeards. He liked calling in turkeys, and when he did, he wanted them to die. I had no problem with his logic. As much as I love to run an Easton through a bird, the old saying that turkeys are made to be shot with a shotgun has some truth to it.

I awoke to thunder and rain battering the window of my tiny Missouri cabin. After slipping into my clothes and collecting my gear, I met Billy in the dining area.

"Not gonna be many turkey hunters out this morning," Billy said. "It's been a while since I've hunted birds in this type of weather. Should make for an interesting morning."

As it turned out, "interesting" was an understatement. The paved road to our hunt area was a river, and twice we debated on whether we should attempt to cross a low point in the road. If Billy hadn't had a monstrous diesel truck, I would've been a lot more reluctant. Going through one of the crossings, we could actually felt the rushing water move the truck a bit. It's amazing what a couple of turkey nuts will risk just to get into the spring woods.

The walk in was sloppy, and, like my buddies and I had in Kansas, we opted for a field-edge set. Neither Billy nor I had been to the property before, so we were simply using the description a local friend had provided and the maps on our phones.

After surveying the field and surrounding timber, which we could barely make out in the inky darkness, we opted to deploy the Double Bull blind on the edge of the field farthest away from the timber.

NOTE: Having never been to the property before, we didn't know where the birds were roosted and we didn't want to risk bumping birds roosted close to or on the field edge. Knowing that any birds in the area would likely hit the field by midmorning and having confidence in our setup—and, of course, Billy's calling—we played it safe and set up well off any possible roost sites. This is a great tip if you're making a morning sit and you're not sure where the birds are roosted. Bump birds off the roost, and you've ruined your day before it has even begun.

BY THE TIME we deployed the blind, the rain had subsided a bit. Not much, but some, and it was nice to be dry and sheltered from the wind. We didn't hear a single gobble on the roost, and there was zero hen talk. We weren't discouraged. Eastern birds have a reputation for getting cement beaks, and bad weather can make them all the quieter. Billy didn't make a peep either. He didn't hammer away on a crow or owl call trying to solicit a shock gobble. We knew from our friend's scouting mission that birds were in the area, and if we remained patient, a bird or two would wander into the field.

As I've mentioned several times in the book, we matched our calling intensity to that of the birds we were hunting. We kept it simple and natural, and it paid off. Ninety minutes after first light, a lone tom walked into the field. He glanced at our full-strut decoy over a laydown hen and came in on a string. Billy didn't call once. There was no reason to. Everything was natural, and we simply let the decoys work for us. Just because he could call (and it's like nothing I've ever heard), didn't mean he should call. Heed this advice.

Somehow the big tom managed to blow up into almost full strut the second he got face to face with our strutter decoy. Billy told me to take him, and I gently squeezed the trigger on his trusty Remington 870. Just like that, another foul-weather tom bit the dust.

I should note that this was the first Eastern bird that paid no attention to the blind. I'm not sure why, but I think the weather could have had something to do with it. Also, there was a rifle shooting tower for deer located only about 15 yards from the ground blind, and this may have helped as well. I still recommend to always brush in your ground blinds whenever possible if you're hunting Eastern birds.

After collecting my Missouri prize and slipping and sliding back to the blind, we opted to stay put for an hour in hopes of pulling off a rainy-day double. We did have another bird wander into the decoys, but it was a hen.

Shortly after the hen inspected our spread and drifted into the timber, the rain stopped and the sun came out. Billy looked at me and I looked at him. The birds had been pounded by the rain and wind for multiple hours, and we knew the change in weather could get them going. It just so happens, it did.

After walking from the field and into the timber, Billy let a few soft yelps slide down into a deep hollow. A tom thundered back immediately, and after losing some elevation and closing the distance on the bird, Billy and I found a couple of big hardwoods and settled in. We were in deep timber and didn't have time to set a decoy, but a decoy wasn't at all necessary.

The bird was gobbling on his own and closing fast, and shortly after Billy let out a few soft purrs, I saw a white head bobbing through the timber. The bird was coming fast, stopping only for a few seconds at time to scan the woods for any sign of the hen. At a distance of 12 yards, Billy's shot was true and our dream of a rainy-day double quickly became reality.

NOTE: Yes, ground blinds are more for the sit-and-wait bowhunter, but when the weather is nasty, nothing is better than having a little shelter. Plus, if you plan on logging some time on a field edge or in the timber, a ground blind allows you to get away with a little more movement and makes things much more comfortable than huddling against a tree or bush for hours.

NOTE: I see too many turkey hunters, both bow and shotgun, get hung up on having to use a decoy. Yes, decoys are great and I prefer them, but when setting up in thick timber, they aren't always necessary. In dense cover, an approaching tom knows that he will likely have to look for his lady love. I've actually had better luck in thick timber sets without decoys, especially when hunting public or pressured private land.

NEBRASKA WIND, Rain, Hail and Snow

If you haven't hunted Nebraska for butterballs yet, you need to add the state to your must-hunt list. Besides the fact that Nebraska is home to a robust population of wild turkeys, it also offers adventurous hunters over 500,000 acres of public land on which to stretch their legs.

Because my home state of Colorado shares a border with

Nebraska and the state offers a March 25 archery-only opener, I tend to kick off my yearly spring turkey tour in the Cornhusker State.

For the past three years I've teamed up with my Nebraska hunting buddy, Terron Bauer, for the opener. Terron and his family are great friends, and hunting their small family farm for a few days each March has become a tradition.

During our three-year early-March span we have hunted a total of six days and have yet to see the sun shine. What we have experienced is rain, hail, snow and gale-force wind. And though the weather has been less than ideal, I have been able to successfully anchor five birds during those six days of hunting. Here's how.

Early-season birds, especially when winter weather looms, are often still in wintertime flocks. You've read about the importance of scouting and putting time in behind the glass, and at no time is heeding this advice more critical than when hunting early-season birds. Be off the "X" by 100 yards or more, and the birds might stroll right past your spread and never give you a look.

NOTE: Toms and jakes traveling with a large group of hens tend to simply follow the girls wherever they go. Because early-season hens are mostly sticking to their wintertime patterns, you need to study those patterns and set up accordingly.

TERRON IS JUST a 20-minute drive from the family farm, and starting in early March, he runs a number of trail cameras on time-lapse mode. This helps him greatly in learning the birds' patterns. In addition to the trail-cam scouting, Terron also logs plenty of hours behind the glass watching when and where birds enter and exit fields.

NOTE: It's crucial when using trail cameras to pattern birds entering and exiting a large field to use models that offer a time-lapse mode. Time lapse records events throughout the day and captures a much wider field of view. The field we hunt in Nebraska each year is quite large, but using our time-lapse camera we can easily monitor the entire field.

LAST SEASON we ventured into the blowing sleet and snow on opening morning. Because I was under the weather with the flu, we were a tad late getting to the field. Not wanting to risk blowing the roost and being spotted as we hurried across the field to our chosen location, we opted to play it safe and hopefully pull a tom or two across the field away from the main group.

Though it was snowing and sleeting, the gobbling action was intense. The birds were hammering on the roost. However, when the first hens hit the field edge and started streaming out toward its middle, the toms and jakes simply followed. There were thirteen gobblers in the group, and not one so much as lifted his head and looked in our direction.

These were totally unpressured birds, but this just goes to show how important it is to be on the "X" when hunting early-season birds.

After the birds exited the field, we moved the blind to the exact spot where the birds had entered the field, which was the exact spot we had planned to get to that morning.

Knowing we had several hours to kill, we went to town to grab lunch and were back in the blind with plenty of time to kill before the birds started working back in our direction.

With two hours of light remaining, as if on cue, the hens entered the field at the exact point they had exited it hours earlier. The mob of forty-plus hens marched into our decoys and got extremely vocal, which fired up the toms. It was one of the coolest things I've ever experienced in the turkey woods. As the hens meandered out of the spread, four gobblers rushed in. In true "Jace fashion" I whiffed on my first chance of the year, shooting under the belly of the biggest tom in the group. The tom was unaware of what had just happened, so I was able to grab a second arrow and make good on my second shot.

Immediately after harvesting my bird, I looked at the wind speed and temperature. The wind was gusting at 22 mph out of the north and the temperature was a gloomy 18 degrees. It just goes to show what can happen when you put in the work and put yourself in the right spot.

NOTE: I love calm, sun-soaked days as much as any turkey hunter, but as previously mentioned, we just don't get many of these each spring. Each year I see too many turkey hunters get caught up in watching the weather and trying to plan each and every hunt around the forecast. You just can't do that, especially if you're making a road trip. You have to simply pick the days you pick and play the cards you're dealt. Not going because the weather is less than ideal simply can't be an option.

6

GOING PUBLIC

I want to start this chapter by telling you that some of my best turkey haunts are found on public ground. That's just a fact, and each and every spring, I seek adventure on open-to-anyone ground.

There is something special about matching wits with wild game on land that is open to anyone. I cut my turkey-hunting teeth chasing public-land birds, and it's a habit I plan, Lord willing, to keep up for many springs to come.

Often, the most difficult part of the public-land turkey equation is simply knowing where to go. And while figuring out where to go isn't as simply as switching on the kitchen light, state game and fish agencies have greatly sped up the learning curve.

Start by going to the game and fish website of the state in which you plan to chase birds. I will use Kansas as an example. After five minutes of surfing the state's website, here are some things I found specifically related to turkey hunting—more importantly, things that will help the adventurous turkey hunter be successful on public land:

- A downloadable Spring Turkey Atlas that shows Walk-In parcels specific to turkeys throughout the state.
- The state has an archery-only turkey season.
- According to the most recent Turkey Brood Survey conducted by state biologists, turkey populations have remained stable across the state but don't seem to be expanding exponentially.
- Average turkey population changes per square mile broken down by county.

AND ALL THIS was gleaned in just five minutes on the state's game and fish site.

Now that you have the general idea of how to get started, let's keep the ball the rolling. The next step is to identify an area that you want to look at more closely. Typically, I pick a couple of counties that border one another and have a significant amount of Walk-In, BLM, etc.

Now it's time to burn up the phone lines to local game wardens and state biologists. I generally skip the game wardens and go right to the biologists. These folks spend their time in the outdoors, and any worth their salt will have a firm grasp on area populations, predation statistics, hatch counts and winter mortality issues. Do yourself a favor before you punch the buttons on your cellphone. Sit down and write out all your questions on a piece of paper. Biologists are busy folks, and if you're prepared and have something more intelligent to say than, "Uh, yeah, I'm coming from out of state and want to know about turkey hunting," you will get a lot more information. I've found the more prepared I am, the more seriously biologists take me and the more willing they are to answer my questions to the fullest. Oh, and don't feel like you're bothering them. These fine folks have folders full of data, and each one I've ever dealt with was only too happy to share some great information.

Here are some basic questions to get you started:

- I'm looking at hunting these specific public areas in (name of county). Do these areas typically hold birds?
- Have the areas experienced any significant die-off?
- How have the most recent hatch counts been?
- Do the properties tend to get a fair amount of pressure?
- Have you personally been on these properties?
- Do you have any good tips for working around the pressure? Is traffic lighter on weekdays? Later in the season?
- I'm not afraid of getting off the beaten path and roaming around. If I go deeper on some of these larger tracts, can I get away from the crowds?
- Are there any areas that aren't on my radar that you would recommend?

THAT LAST QUESTION IS A BIGGIE. Over the years I have had a total of twelve different properties in four different states recommended to me by biologists. Each one of them proved to be a killer spot, and to this day I still find birds on them.

With a little time and research, you can string together your own list of public hot spots.

Now that you've interviewed a biologist or two and have narrowed your search further, it's time to go digital. Yes, I'm a fan of Google Earth, and I do like the fact that I can change the date range to spring and take an aerial look at the locales I plan to inspect. However, in my opinion, onX Maps (www.onxmaps.com) trumps Google Earth and most other mapping systems I've used. The aerial image is clear, you can easily see the public borders, and you can mark spots you plan to inspect. Marking spots is huge. Doing so gives you a massive advantage upon arrival.

So what are some of the things you're looking for when digital scouting? Personally, I like to locate waterways dotted with large trees. In addition to noting a few likely roosting sites, it's super important to note possible strut zones and feeding areas. After fly-down, mature toms usually like to move to areas where they can make themselves visible to hens. Open meadows, clear-cuts in the timber, logging roads and fields are great areas to take note of. I also like to locate areas pressured birds are likely to go. Pay close attentions to deep hollows and heavy timber bordering private land.

If I'm hunting mountain Merriam's, I tend to look for long ridges dotted with ponderosa pines. If those ridges feed into open meadows, it's all the better. In addition, especially when hunting Merriam's, I like to contact the local forest service office and find the current elevation of the snow line. As previously mentioned, Merriam's birds love to follow that melting snow line as it moves up the mountain.

OK, you've done your research and your maps are marked. You can take a breather, but you're not even close to done. If you want to have a pleasant public-land hunt, there are still a lot of logistics to figure out.

I'm a tightwad, and motels and restaurants cost money. I like to road trip on a budget, and honestly, for me, camping and cooking outside adds to the whole experience. A pull-behind camper is great, but tent camping works too, and that's the route I take most often. I like that camping keeps me close to the action. Most of the areas I hunt are at least a thirty-minute drive one way from the nearest town, and I hate driving back and forth. Plus, staying close saves on gas. Just make sure you check to see that the area you're looking at allows camping before you show up with your tent or camper. If it doesn't, it's likely there's a state park, KOA or other camping facility nearby.

When it comes to food, I recommend taking some with you in coolers. My wife is wonderful and prepares a ton of meals for me beforehand. That way all I have to do after a long day in the field is turn on my camp stove and heat up a hot meal. I also take all of my own snacks and drinks. Having food ready at camp eliminates the urge to run to a restaurant, which keeps more gas in the tank and more money in your wallet.

Having spent months planning a public-land adventure it's hard not to rush into the woods upon arrival, especially when you have a limited number of days to hunt. However, I highly recommend resisting the temptation. Typically, I try to arrive midday regardless of whether the season is already open or opens the next day. I do a little Jedi mind trick and don't count this afternoon as one of my hunt days. Telling myself it's not a hunt day keeps me from making a stupid, unnecessary move. Instead, I spend the afternoon driving the perimeter of the area or areas I plan to hunt. So many times, even on heavily pressured land, I've spied birds out in the open or in an adjacent private-land field.

After taking a little cruise, I put boots on the ground but am super careful not to penetrate too deeply and blow birds out. Instead, I walk logging roads and search for sign (turkeys leave a pile of sign). A few tracks, feathers and droppings are all I need to see. I never call; I don't even hack away on a locator call. Even if it's opening day, I always go into any public-land situation like the birds I'm hunting have been under severe pressure. Instead of calling, I listen. Countless times while walking logging roads, my ears have detected faint hen talk and booming gobbles.

As evening draws near and my plan for the next day's hunt continues to percolate, I move to an area where I can look over a vast amount of ground. By now, I typically have a solid idea of where a few likely roost sites are, and I spend the remaining part of my day trying to spy a tom or two as they meander toward their sleeping grounds. If the area you're hunting isn't the best for visibility, don't fret. Just get to a high point and listen. Chances are you'll hear birds as they sound off on their way to roost.

NOTE: If you don't happen to spy a single turkey during your scouting foray and don't see any go to roost, don't get discouraged. Turkeys are elusive creatures, and countless times I've gone to bed thinking I wouldn't have a bird to hunt in the morning only to be serenaded by gobbles as I set up in the morning's inky blackness.

In addition, I've hunted all day on public tracts and not seen or heard a single bird, and then found myself the following morning not knowing which way to go due to intense on-the-roost gobbling. Remember, during the course of a day, turkeys eat, walk, loaf and breed. That's basically it. It's not uncommon for a given area to be lukewarm one day and red hot the next, especially if an adjoining property, whether private or public, receives some pressure.

OK, it's time to get the show on the road and start hunting for birds. Here's what you need to do in order to come out of the woods with a fan bobbing behind your head.

Morning Sits ... Know Your Competition

Every other hunter in the area is competition, and much like a college coach studies his opponent, you must predict the likely habits of other hunters in the area. Remember, most hunters, whether they are toting a shotgun or a bow, will opt for a field-edge set first thing in the morning. If during your scouting you spied other hunters glassing the same field birds you did, make a morning plan that is opposite theirs. Yes, I know it's hard to give up the field-edge option, but I would much rather not be blind to blind with other hunters.

If the birds are roosted right on the field edge, don't put an unethical plan into action. Instead, use your brain and the lay of the land to predict where the birds will go after leaving the field. Oftentimes, I figure this out in my tent at night while looking at onX. Solid options include meadows and other openings in the timber where toms can continue to strut for the girls.

If the hens leave the boys after exiting the field, toms will begin to wander and will often sound off. Oftentimes, I simply watch from a distance and move in accordingly after the birds exit the field. If the birds aren't pressured and slide by the other hunters, I note their direction of travel and head for openings where I can deploy my blind and decoys. If the birds do receive pressure, I typically head for the deep timber, set up my blind and listen. It might take an hour or two, but I will usually either hear or see birds. I've had some of my most successful hunts after watching birds get blown out of a field. Remember, don't ever panic. Public-land hunting is tough, especially with a bow. Keep your head screwed on and your wits about you, and you'll often find yourself in the action.

If the birds are roosted well off the field, it's fine to slip into the timber—or better yet a sizeable opening—they are likely to cross through before hitting the field. This doesn't mean to put this plan into motion if the birds are only 100 yards off the field edge. I only slip between roosted birds and other hunters if I know for certain the birds arc at least half a mile away from where other hunters are set up. Yes, public land is public land, but as Ron Burgundy so eloquently put it in *Anchorman,* "Let's keep it classy."

On the flip side, if you struck gold and believe you're likely to have a public field to yourself, by all means, deploy the field-edge set up. Remember, stay off the roost and let your decoys and calls work. Be set up well before the break of day. You don't want to be wandering around in a field and get picked off by the eyes of roosted birds. Over the years I've seen way too many bowhunters pushing the limits. It starts getting late in the hunt and the odds of success seem impossible. They've been hunting hard and finally have the right setup, but they just can't get out of the tent in the morning a few minutes earlier. Don't let this be you.

My favorite spread for a public-land field-edge set includes a single ¾-strut jake, a laydown hen and a feeding hen placed off to one side. I'll use a full-strut tom early and late in the turkey rut, but the aforementioned is my go-to. Again, be sure to leave space between the jake and the laydown hen so an approaching tom can walk between them. If I'm bowhunting, I prefer to put my decoys no farther than 15 yards. If I'm toting a shotgun, my preferred distance is 30 yards.

Why the strutter early and late? Early in the season it's common to see gobblers running together, and they often won't hesitate to come beat up on a loner. Later in the season, dominant birds are still looking to breed, and if an older mature gobbler sees another tom near a potentially receptive hen, he will often come in.

As far as calling, if I put the birds to bed and know only a single tom or two occupies the roost, I always let them do the talking first. Typically, if the weather is at all decent, lonely toms will start gobbling even before the first rays of morning arrive. Don't freak out the second you hear one sound off in the predawn darkness and fire back with a series of yelps. Just relax and listen. If a tom is gobbling before the break of day, you can typically bank on the fact that he'll gobble more as light spills across the landscape.

This is a great time to put your binos to work. Scan the nearby trees to see if you can spot the noisemakers and study their body language. Are they strutting on the limb? Which direction are they facing when they gobble? Are their heads moving about like they're starting to scan for other birds? What colors are their heads? Remember, white means he's ultra-fired up. Once you get a feel for their mood, keep listening to the gobbling.

Oftentimes, through my optics, I've been able to tell that roosted birds see my spread. Yes, optics are important for the turkey hunter. If the tom or toms in the tree have their heads turned in your direction and are gobbling, chances are your decoys are doing their job. At this point, I generally either let out only a couple of hen yelps or simply stay quiet. Again, I like to listen. I like to keep my ears tuned to the woods and see if I can detect any distant or close-by hen talk. If I hear a hen or two nearby, I will start by mimicking the noise the live hens are producing. I want to make sure I keep the toms' interest, and don't lose them to the seductive talk of live hens. If the hens are distant, I keep watching the body language of the boy birds. If the birds start turning on the limb and gobbling in the direction of the distant ladies, I will let out some soft yelps, clucks and purrs to remind them that there are willing girls closer. If I can't see the birds on the limb, I follow the same rules above. I listen and then respond.

NOTE: Keep in mind that when hunting early-season birds, your chances of spying them on the roost are much better due to the lack of foliage. As the spring season progresses and trees begin to leaf out, it becomes harder and harder to spot birds on the limb.

IF I SEE ONLY a single tom roosted with ladies, or hear what I believe to be a single tom roosted with a few hens, my approach changes drastically. A single tom roosted with one or more girls typically isn't looking to spark a new romance. Most often that tom will follow his live ladies wherever they go. How long that tom will stick to those hens depends on the phase of the rut. Early on, he may stay with them all day. As the season progresses and his bred hens move off to tend their nests, he may only court them for a short period before going walk-about.

Regardless of the time of year, it is very possible to kill a tom roosted with one or more hens. The key is calling to the hens. As morning dawns and the hens start to let out a few tree yelps, I will follow suit, but will try not to be ultra-vocal. I just want the girls to know that there are some new ladies in town that, if given the chance, would love to steal their boy wonder.

As light increases, one or more of the hens will start yelping and even cutting. When this happens, I go right back at her. My goal is to piss one or more of the ladies in the group off and get them to come my way. If the hens fly down toward my fakes and start marching my way, I get silent. I only call again if they deviate from their course or hang up for more than a minute or two. If the hens commit, the tom will follow.

Oftentimes, especially during the early season, I find multiple toms and numerous hens in a given roost site. Most often, there will be a couple of dominant three- and four-year-olds in the group. These birds will typically be the ones that stick with their hens. My goal becomes enticing a lovesick two-year-old bird to fly down and come join my party.

Once the birds pitch down, it's common for the more dominant gobblers to start pushing their hens away, or for the hens to pull their men away. If you notice a couple of birds that linger behind, often facing your spread and gobbling, those are your two-year-old birds. They should be your focus.

Midmorning to Midday

If my morning field-edge plan is a bust, I simply take note of the direction the birds worked and then try and slip around them. It's important not to take up the trail of the birds as you would if you were tracking a wounded deer. You don't want to tail the birds and sneak up on them. You want to loop around them and get where you think they're going.

If you've done your scouting, you should have a few likely places in mind. For me, these locales include logging roads, large sandy openings, sage-dappled flats, small openings surrounded by thick cover and open meadows with abundant bug life near water.

If you don't have a place in mind, pull out your smartphone, bring up Google Earth or onX, and start prospecting. What I like to do is note on the map where the birds exited the field and then take a look at the surrounding landscape. Oftentimes, the right place to move to practically smacks you right in the face.

NOTE: As I've mentioned, onX is my go-to mapping tool. What I like is the fact that it will work without cellular service. All you need to do is download your maps ahead of time, and you can then pull those maps up on your phone and view them even when you don't have service. Your current location will still be marked as well.

AS I PUT my midmorning to midday plan to action, I'm always on the lookout for something better. You don't want to get tunnel vision. Don't mark a spot on your map and go marching at Mach 10 toward it. Stay sharp and flexible. Many times, while moving toward my planned location, I relocate the birds from the morning or stumble into new birds. Obviously when this happens, my plans change. And even if I don't stumble into birds, I often find a spot that gets my spidey sense tingling. If and when this happens, don't fight it. Stop and set up.

Regardless of whether you make it to your pre-planned destination or alter your plan, once you deploy the blind, stay put. I've called more turkeys between 10 a.m. and 3 p.m. than I can shake a stick at. In fact, it's my favorite time of day to hunt. We will get to why in a minute.

NOTE: It can be difficult to brush in a blind on a field edge. I still try, but the lack of cover can make it tough. However, unless there is simply no time, I always brush in my pop-up hide during my midmorning to midday sits. Is it necessary? Not always, but I would rather be safe than sorry. You have the time, so do the work. I've had many Eastern birds, a couple of Merriam's and several Rios take note of a blind that wasn't brushed in. Most of these birds were crafty public-land dwellers, but a few Easterns reacted to blinds on private ground, too.

The good news when it comes to brushing in a turkey blind is that it doesn't take much. You don't have to get whitetail-crazy. Tuck it against a tree or bush, add some side and front cover, and you're set. Remember, in some states it is illegal to trim branches and other vegetation on public ground. Always check state game laws before hacking away. If it is illegal, you can often find plenty of debris already on the ground.

After I get my blind set and brushed in, I get out all of my necessary gear and just sit in silence for a few minutes. I like to let things calm down, and oftentimes I will hear a distant yelp or gobble. Sometimes, when Lady Luck really shines on me, I get lucky and hear a close gobble.

After a few minutes of sitting in silence, if I've haven't

heard or seen any birds, I start with some light calling. No, I don't start cutting and going bonkers. I just let out a few soft yelps, pause, and then let out a louder yelp or two. Next, I listen for a response. If I get none, I simply sit quietly for another 15 to 20 minutes and then repeat the process. The key is not getting frustrated and not picking up and moving. Remember, turkeys have nothing to do during the course of the day but walk, eat, breed and loaf. Stay focused and stay committed.

More times than not, I will have been in my blind for a few hours doing my same little calling sequence and starting to get bored out of my mind when a tom strolls into the decoys without making a peep. Sometimes—and this is my favorite—I go through my series of calls and a tom shatters my eardrums because he is so close to the blind. Gosh, that gets me going!

When I'm hunting public land, I would say that eight times out of ten if I'm patient and commit to a midmorning to midday spot, I have at least one bird show up. I don't always kill that bird and it's not always a tom, but those odds are pretty dang high and I will take them any day. It can get monotonous and the urge to head back to camp tends to grow with each passing hour, but you must resist. What are you going to do at camp? Yep, the same thing you're doing in your blind: nothing. The difference is you have a chance to kill a bird in your blind. I always have a book or two with me, and this is a great way to pass the time. It's also a good idea to have a portable phone charger. When the blind crazies start, you'll be texting everyone you know.

Now for the reason this is my favorite time of day to hunt spring birds: toms love to wander, and if I get a gobble after 10 a.m., my odds of calling in that bird and getting off a shot are really, really good. Plus, I just love the anticipation. I've conditioned my mind to believe that there are likely birds close by, and I will eventually have one respond, magically appear or see it in the distance. And you know what? Most of the time, my belief becomes reality.

The only time I move when sitting in a ground blind or natural hide (we will talk more about natural hides later) is if I'm convinced the birds have found a loafing area, I can hear them talking and I'm certain the chatter is coming from the same place. If this is the case, I will take a risk and move in.

NOTE: It's extremely frustrating to be sitting in the spot you committed to and have another hunter come ambling through. Yes, it sucks, but it does happen. The key is staying focused to your plan. You can't control what others are doing, but you can control what you do and how you respond. It can be easy to just pack up the blind and move, but I almost always stay. Why? Simple. Experience has taught me to do so. During my turkey-hunting tenure, I've had a total of four hunters walk past my blind during my midmorning to midday sits. I stayed put on three of the four occasions. Each of those three times I ended up killing a bird less than two hours after losing sight of the other hunter. The one time I did move was because the hunter had poor ethics and set his ground blind 43 yards from mine.

NOTE: Though I'm not in love with hunting in deep, thick timber, I have had some great success in these locales. The reason I'm not a fan is because my visibility is limited, and because I often bowhunt, my shooting windows are often hindered as well. However, deep timbered bottoms, hollows or whatever you call them in your neck of the woods are a great place to get away from people and are top-notch places for duping pressured birds.

Midday to Dark

This is a tricky time frame, but I love it. Many turkey hunters I know call it quits late in the afternoon and return to camp. Not me. If my midmorning to midday plan doesn't produce, I will pick up and loop cautiously around to the field I hunted that morning. If the field looks free of competition, I will set up right where I saw the birds exit hours earlier. No, I don't want to get right on the roost, but I don't mind being within a couple hundred yards of it. If the birds weren't pressured, chances are good they might return on the same route, and you will be ready and waiting.

Typically, when hunting field edges during the evening, I don't call much. I put all my chips into what I know: the birds were there that morning, nothing bothered them, they walked out of the field unalarmed and there is a good chance they will be back. Even if I hear a tom fire away in the distance, I will often keep the calls in the vest.

Once the birds hit the field, I will only call if they aren't working my way. If they are just moving along naturally and working in my direction, I continue to stay quiet.

If the evening field setup doesn't produce, you must stay in your blind until darkness completely swallows the landscape. You don't want to alarm roosted birds, and it's likely you will want to hunt the birds again the following morning. Yes, at this point you're tired, frustrated and likely a little annoyed. How can a bird with the brain the size of a pea be so hard to kill, right? However, you must not give in to pessimistic thoughts. Stay put and get out of the area quietly after dark.

Yes, it is possible to kill a bird late in the day without being on a field. It happens every year. A lot. My favorite midday to dark sits include transition areas in the timber or a small opening where birds are likely to travel through on their way back to roost. My favorite technique, though, is to find a funnel. Yes, much like we do for whitetail. Birds love to funnel through narrow pinches of timber, and if you can find one near a known roost, you'll likely be in the chips. Another advantage to not being on a field is that you can get out of Dodge a little earlier and get back to camp.

7

LATE-SEASON PUBLIC-LAND GOBBLERS

One of my favorite times to hunt public-land gobblers is during the late season. Depending on which state I'm hunting, this time frame is typically from May 15 to May 30. Yes, the birds have been pressured, and every Tom, Dick and Harry has burned boot leather on public tracts and squawked on every call imaginable, but most of the time these public tracts are ghost towns during the late season. I don't mind hunting pressured birds when I'm not competing with other hunters.

My favorite late-season turkey tactic is to scout, scout and scout some more. By this point in the season, most hens have been bred and many are sitting on nests. My goal is to try to locate a few gobblers in the area and take their temperature. If I find toms feeding leisurely together, not blowing up into strut often and basically relaxing, I know the rut has seriously progressed and my plan for killing these birds shouldn't involve aggressive calling. Instead, if I have a few days to hunt, I take a single day and dedicate it to keeping tabs on these birds. Of course, my bow is always with me, and if I get a chance to loose an arrow during my scouting foray, I jump at it, but it has to be a darn good chance.

Now, I realize you won't be able to keep tabs on birds throughout the day. They will move into the timber and the like, but if they've been pressured, chances are they won't roam about much. After I lose sight of the birds I'm watching, I circle around, either by foot or in my vehicle, and try to gain another glassing point. I just make sure not to bump them. If I can locate the birds again, great. If I can't, I head to another piece of property and start prospecting, but I make sure to be back in enough time to try to locate the birds again in late afternoon.

Once I get a good feel for what the birds are doing, I move in for the kill. If you've done your homework and know right where to set up, the odds are in your favor. Brush your blind in well and set out the most realistic fakes you have. If the spot is small enough, I will often go without decoys and just wait for the birds to give me a drive-by. The key is to make every effort to make the scene appear as natural as possible. If I do use decoys and my scouting has told me the toms aren't acting rutty, I will typically use a couple of feeding hens and a jake. Just remember, when hunting pressured birds, your chances decrease greatly each time you go in and out of an area. Your goal is to kill on your first trip in. This is why I put so much emphasis on scouting.

There have been multiple times late in the season when I've found several boisterous gobblers still actively looking to breed hens. While I like finding these birds more than laidback birds, it's still very important to spend time scouting and make your first attempt your best attempt.

Regardless of where I decide to sit, I try to keep the calling to an extreme minimum. No matter how excited the toms are getting, I always remind myself that these birds have likely been called at multiple times. This is where having mastery of the calls you plan to use pays off in spades. Keep the sounds as original as possible, and keep the calling soft, subtle and yelp-free. Let me elaborate. It's super rare for me to cut or do any excited yelping on late-season public dirt. Rather, I use single yelps, clucks and purrs—just enough to keep a tom interested—and count on my decoys to do the rest.

If tom behavior tells me the birds are still somewhat aggressive, I go with a full-strut tom and a single hen decoy. Why the strutter at this point in the season? Most two-year-old birds have had their butts handed to them multiple times, and are often reluctant to come even to a jake decoy. Many of the mature toms have passed on their genes, and a full-strut decoy is super visual and often tells the onlooker that the hen the strutter is guarding is still willing to breed. If the bird is a dominant bird, he's likely to come. If my strutter/hen combo doesn't get much attention or seems to bother other boy birds, I immediately switch to just a pair of hens. On multiple occasions, especially when bowhunting a field edge, I've had a tom wonder bowhunting-close to hen-only decoys.

I'm also a big fan during the late season of no-decoy sits in tight timber. It's common for pressured public-land birds to seek sanctuary by heading into the deep timber. If the tract is big enough, the birds will move as far away from access points as possible. Believe me, the birds you're hunting know the area they call home very well. They know where hunting pressure comes from and are aware of locations where they're likely to get themselves in trouble. Many times, during the late season, I find the biggest piece of public dirt I can find and note access points. I also look at how I would have hunted the property in the early season and then use this information to triangulate where I believe the birds are holing up.

If I find a spot and can scout it, great. If not, I take my blind and decoys just in case and head straight to the remote areas I've identified. Of course, I take my time and keep a keen eye and ear peeled on my way in. If I find turkey sign in thick areas, I pop up my blind and leave the decoys in the bags. Some of my best late-season bowhunts for public-land birds have come by simply circling a spot on a map and going in.

8

ARCHERY TURKEY GEAR & PROPER PRACTICE

As with any type of bowhunting, chasing turkeys with a stick and string requires quality gear, although if you're a bowhunter, you will likely already possess a lot of it. Check out the simplified list below.

Bow

You don't need to change a thing for turkeys. The rig you shoot for big game will be just fine. However, because I shoot so much and want to preserve my shoulders, I do turn my poundage down from 70 to 60 pounds. Turkeys are thin-skinned and light-boned. The only concern is their countless feathers that can hinder a broadhead—fixed or expandable—and kill penetration. Luckily, you don't need much penetration to kill a bird, and I actually prefer a broadhead that remains in the bird.

Worried about turning down you bow? Don't be. All the years I pulled 70 pounds for turkeys, I didn't get any more pass-throughs than I do pulling 60 pounds. Do yourself a favor and turn the bow down. Of course, you're going to want to be sure that bow is outfitted with a rest, sight, quiver and stabilizer. When it comes to the choice of accessories you put on your rig, it's totally up to you. Whatever you use for deer and other big game will work just fine for spring-time birds.

ARROW

My turkey arrow of choice is the same arrow I shoot pronghorn, elk and deer with. I don't change a thing. I have a serious love affair with Easton's 5MM Full Metal Jacket shafts. They hit hard, fly like darts and are super easy to remove from any target. My total arrow weight is 476 grains, which my Prime bow, turned down to 60 pounds, propels at 260 fps. When that shaft hits feathers, it's hitting with 71.44 pounds of kinetic energy, which is more than enough for turkey. Could I gain a little more speed by lightening up my arrow? Sure, but my average shot on turkeys is 13 yards. Top pin, baby!

BROADHEAD

So far, I haven't mentioned anything you should actually have to run out and purchase, unless of course you are new to bowhunting. However, when it comes to broadheads, I really feel some are much better for turkeys than others. It's fine if you live in the fixed-blade camp, but when it comes to springtime butterballs, you really should migrate over and join us in mechanical land for a few months. Turkeys are small targets, and their vitals are even smaller. Regardless of which way a bird is facing (we will discuss those angles later in this book), you can bank on needing to put your shaft in a spot that is slightly smaller than the circumference of a baseball. This is why I highly recommend a large-cutting expandable like Rage's 2-Blade Hypodermic Trypan. This head flies like a field point, boasts a 2-inch cutting diameter and is murder on birds. Other tried-and-true turkey mechanicals that have earned a place in my quiver include G5's DeadMeat and NAP's KillZone. When you're shooting a large-cutting mechanical, you have a little more wiggle room should you miss the mark.

BLIND

If you want to be a run-and-gun turkey hunter and not spend time in a ground blind, that's your business, but you will almost certainly kill a lot more birds from a pop-up ground blind than you will trying to stalk springtime birds. The only run-and-gun tactic I use for turkeys when bowhunting is a bow-mounted decoy. (More on this later.) The reason for this is simple: I like to be out in nature and call birds in close.

When it comes to my choice of blind, only one will do, and that's the Double Bull from Primos. Stay away from smaller blinds. Sure, you can save some greenbacks and go smaller. You can also save some money by purchasing a blind that is the same size as a Double Bull, but you'll be sacrificing quality, durability and function. A sound invest-ment like a Double Bull means comfort, easy set-up and longevity. I've used my Double Bull Bullpen for four seasons now, and it has yet to fail me. In addition, I'm also a big fan of the new Double Bull SurroundView 360. Launched in 2018, this ground fortress boasts one-way see-through walls that allow you to see your surroundings without being seen. With this blind, you can see all those quiet gobblers that come sneaking in from behind the blind. Plus, it's just fun. You feel so exposed, but the birds can't see a thing.

BLIND CHAIR

There are some great chairs on the market today, and as with my blind, I don't skimp on quality. If I'm packing in on public land, I prefer the Primos Tri Stool. This chair will cost you less than a $50 bill and weighs less than 7 pounds. The triangular seat shape is great for leg circulation, and the flared backrest promises support. If I'm hunting private land or an area where I simply leave a blind all season long, I opt for the Swivel Tri Stool from Primos or the Roost Chair from ALPS OudoorZ. Both offer 360 degrees of movement and have multiple adjustments to ensure you can achieve a customized fit.

DECOYS

I've watched guys stand in the turkey decoy aisle at Bass Pro Shops, Cabela's, Scheels and Sportsman's Warehouse and go bat-crap crazy. Why? Because there are so many decoy options on the market today. Let me simplify it for you. Are you ready? Good. Remember these brands and you'll be just fine: Dave Smith Decoys and Avian-X. My favorites are Dave Smith fakes, and the only reason for that is I've had some durability trouble with Avian's inflatable line. Though these blow-up decoys are great for packing in, I have had some issues with the valve systems. That said, I wouldn't be at all afraid to invest my hard-earned coin on these decoys. They look incredible, are easy to pack and Avian sent me brand-new models when I experienced trouble.

The DSDs are as solid as they come. Dave Smith is an artist, and sometimes it just doesn't seem fair to have such realistic decoys out in front of me. The DSDs are harder to pack, but they are built like tanks. Regardless of which way you decided to go, I would recommend a jake, a laydown hen and a feeder hen. Over time, you can invest in a strutter, but I use my hen combo with a jake all year long and it has proven effective.

CALLS

We've touched on this a little but not nearly enough. Calling, for me, is what makes turkey hunting such a blast. My advice is to buy a number of diaphragm calls from a number of different manufacturers and see what you like. My favorite cuts are the standard-V, shipwreck, bat-wing, ghost cut and double-cut. When it comes to the manufacturers I stick with, the list is short but distinguished. It includes Zink, Primos, M.A.D., Quaker Boy and Rocky Mountain. In addition to your diaphragms, I also recommend visiting a quality sporting goods store—one that will let you play with various pot-and-peg and box calls—and do a little field-testing. When it comes to pot-and-peg, I always have them in the following surfaces: slate, aluminum and glass. As for box calls, I'm old school and really like the sound I get when I run a standard call that requires chalk on the paddle and rails. I do have one that requires no chalk and can be run in wet weather, but I rarely use it. I also carry a hawk-screech locater call. I prefer to make owl hoots with my mouth, but if you can't, this is a must-have locater as well. I also carry a dried turkey wing—simply cut one off a bird you kill—to simulate both fly-down and toms fighting. Lastly, I carry a gobbler shaker so I can effectively make the sound of a male bird.

Of course, there are a number of other gear items you will come across, and whether you decide to add them to your turkey arsenal or not is up to you. This gear advice is just meant to put you in the game and provide the basic, essential tools you will need in the turkey woods.

Becoming a 5 Percenter

It's often said, when it comes to big game hunting, that 10 percent of the bowhunters kill 90 percent of the game. I agree. When it comes to consistently killing turkeys with archery tackle and making clean and effective kills, I believe that 10 percent slips down to 5 percent. Why? Because, according the journal that I write in religiously, over the past ten turkey seasons I've been present for thirty-eight clean misses and twenty-four wounded birds that were never recovered. I know nobody likes to talk about real numbers when it comes to misses and lost game, but if we want to be real about things, we simply must. Three of those clean misses are mine, and, sadly, I own four of those lost birds as well. I hate it, but I own it, and I've taken great lengths to ensure that I make a clean, quick kill each and every time.

When it comes to becoming a turkey killer with archery tackle, it's important to have a system. Target panic, turkey fever—whatever you want to label it—comes when a system breaks down. Here's the bad news: It's going to take some time to build your system. Here's the good news: Once you do, it will forever change your bowhunting life.

How you build your system is up to you, and there are

many routes you can take. Personally, I took the advice of my good buddy Phil Mendoza, a champion archer and pro shop owner, and sprinkled in things of my own along the way. If you want to check out Phil's system, visit www.alpha-bowhunting.teachable.com, locate course 2.0 Bowhunting Building Blocks —Buck Fever and Target Panic, and get going.

If you're just looking to wing it, let me help you a little. Shooting hundreds of arrows a day isn't going to get you over the target panic/turkey fever hump. There is simply no way to prepare for those anxiety-filled, heart-thumping moments that come when a critter wanders bowhunting-close. However, if you develop a system that starts with how you grip your bow and ends with a perfectly released arrow, your muscle memory will simply take over even when your heart rate redlines. Before you start developing your system, I highly recommend that you purchase a tension release. Not a hinge release, but a tension release. My go-to is the PerfeX Resistance from Stanislawski.

The beauty of a tension or resistance release is it allows you to settle in at full draw, hit your anchor, unlock the release by letting go of your thumb handle and then use back tension to fire it. Basically, it's a simpler way to shoot a back-tension release because there is no rotation involved and there is no worry about punching yourself in the nose during the draw cycle.

This release causes you to focus on your target and simply won't let you punch the trigger the second your pin floats on foam. As you develop your system and learn to let your pin float around the area you want your arrow to impact, you will find your accuracy will reach a level you never thought possible. Plus, your mind won't be screaming at you to go into launch mode. Rather, you will get to a point where letting your pin float on a spot is almost relaxing, and before you know it, the shot will just happen. It's an amazing feeling, and I truly hope everyone reading this book can get there.

As I mastered and got comfortable with my tension release and learned to trust my system, I made the switch to a hinge- or back-tension release. You may or may not do this. You may choose to hunt with your tension-style release aid or go back to your thumb-activated or index-finger release. I tried to go back, but the feeling wasn't the same. Even though I'd mastered my system, on occasion I still would hammer my trigger. So I went the hinge route and will never look back. I've learned that if I execute every step of my system, every single shot I make with a hinge release is a good shot. This past season, I went four for four on turkeys, and each arrow was 10-ring perfect. Twice I was certain my shot was going to be off. I felt like I was all over the place, but when it broke, my projectile was right where it needed to be. Again, I'm not saying a hinge is the hunting release everyone should use. I have a buddy who built a solid system using Phil's plan. Last year he was five for five on big game animals, and not once did he punch his index release.

Of course, you're going to need to spend time on the range. The beautiful thing about archery is that it takes the same perfect form to make a perfect shot at 10 yards as it does at 80 yards. For this reason, I frequently practice in my backyard where the maximum shooting distance is 20 yards. When I practice in the backyard my focus isn't on the number of arrows I shoot, but rather on making sure each and every arrow is perfect. Now, perfect doesn't mean a 12-ring. You must wrap your head around this: perfect means following your system to the letter and executing the best shot you possibly can. I've found when I heed this advice, my arrow is right where it needs to be more often than not.

Typically, my backyard sessions happen three times per week, and on average I shoot between eight and thirteen arrows per session. Why? Because perfect practice makes perfect. Champion archer, Mathews Archery Pro Shooter and Director of Marketing for T.R.U. Ball Brandon Reyes once told me, "It's not about how much you shoot. In fact, shooting too much can actually be a bad thing. It's all about making every shot you take perfect. I would rather shoot five perfect arrows than a hundred just to say I shot my bow a hundred times."

Besides being great for mastering your system and focusing on flawless execution, backyard shooting sessions are also perfect for practicing effective turkey shot angles you can expect to take in the field. Years ago, I purchased Rinehart's Tom Turkey 3-D target, and though I've gone through a few replaceable vital sections, this decoy has held up really well. I only use it in the months leading up to spring, and I can easily position the decoy at the various effective kill angles I know I need to practice. Here are those angles.

Facing Toward You

This is a tough shot, especially if the bird is in strut and full of air. The room for error is small, and you will want to make sure to focus your pin just above the bird's beard. Hit this spot, and the bird is dead. Miss high, and you have a good chance of hitting the neck, which is also a fatal shot. Hit the bird much below the beard, and you will be in for a long day.

FACING AWAY From You

This is my favorite shot on a turkey when the bird is not in strut. Simply hold in the middle of the bird's back and execute. Your shot will often sever the spine and hit a number of vital organs as it passes through and punches out the bird's chest. If the bird is in strut, the base of the fan offers an ideal aiming point. The arrow will pass through the bird's intestines and guts before continuing through the chest. A bird hit in the "vent" won't go far.

QUARTERING Toward You

Turkeys don't have heavy bones, and while we often shy away from quartering-to shots on big game, we can go ahead and take a turkey at this angle. Simply draw a horizontal line from the bird's beard, then draw a vertical line up from the bird's offside leg. When your vertical line intersects your horizontal line, you're good. This shot will take out the bird's heart, and if you hit high, your arrow will hit the spine. If the bird is in strut, move your horizontal line about two inches below the base of the neck and move your vertical line a few inches forward from the offside leg.

BROADSIDE

The main thing with this shot is focusing on not hitting the bird low. This happens a lot when a turkey is in strut. It's easy to hold low and execute the shot. Just remember, hit em' low and watch em' go. If the bird is not in strut, focus on where the wing butt goes into the body and come back from the wing butt about two inches. If the bird is in strut, the crease you need to hit will be easily disguisable in the upper-wing area.

Head/Neck Shot

The cool thing about this shot is there is zero doubt about where to aim, and if you hit the head or neck, the bird will drop in its tracks. The problem with this shot is that the bird's head will often be moving. Make sure the head is still before executing your shot.

Twice a week, sometimes more if I can find the time, I head to my local 3-D range and loose some arrows at realistic targets. At my small course, I can shoot a total of seven targets, and I typically shoot the course three times. When shooting 3-D, I always record my score from each session in my journal. Each time, I try to better my score. As with my backyard sessions, I focus on releasing perfect arrows. If I hit a 5 on a target or even whiff, I simply move on to the next target. I've learned that if I don't, I will shoot another arrow and then another at the same target. Typically, those shots will be rushed. Plus, in the bowhunting woods, you typically only get one chance to make the shot.

If there's no one at the range, and there usually isn't, I practice shooting several targets at different distances. Typically, I really like to stretch things out. Yes, turkeys will likely be close, but if I can hammer 3-D targets out to 100 yards and I stick to my system, those 12-yard shots are all the easier.

I often take a few buddies with me to the range. We all take a few dollars and create a little competition. Not only is this fun, but shooting around others can elevate the heart rate. It's easy to trust our system when we're alone, but adding a few sets of eyes as you go through your system can recreate some of those in-the-field nerves. It's also good to enter a few 3-D tournaments. Typically, I shoot indoor 3-D tournaments in the winter and outdoor events in the spring.

Here are a few more shooting tips to keep in mind. Practice them often.

- Whether in the backyard or on the range, be sure to shoot often from the chair you plan to sit in.
- If you're going to use a bow-mounted decoy, don't let the first time you shoot with it on your bow be at a turkey. A bow-mounted decoy will give your bow a different feel, and you will need to practice with it often.
- Take time at dawn, midday and dusk to shoot some arrows from your ground blind. Shooting at different times of the day allows you to see how well your pin illuminates in a blind. Plus, shooting from your blind will teach you about arrow clearance. Don't join the "I Shot The Blind" Club.

9

BE A RUN-AND-GUNNER

If the thought of sitting in a blind day after day for hours on end makes you feel nauseated, you may want to consider a different approach. And if you're normally all about the blind but want to get out and roam around a little, consider the run-and-gun option.

Here's what I've discovered when running and gunning with my bow: it's hard, and it often does more harm than good unless you have a bow-mounted decoy. Have I pulled off the occasional spot-and-stalk without a bow-mounted decoy during the spring? Yes, but they have been few and far between, and more often than not, I end up blowing whatever piece of property I'm hunting.

When it comes to using a bow-mounted decoy, I prefer the Heads-Up Strutting Turkey Decoy from Heads-Up Decoy or the Ultimate Predator Gear's Turkey Decoy. Both mount easily to the bow—the Ultimate Predator to the riser via Velcro and the Heads-Up to the stabilizer using an included mounting system. I really like how the Ultimate Predator Turkey Decoy wraps around the bow's riser, but when it comes to pure realism, I like being able to add my own fan to my Heads-Up Strutting Turkey Decoy. I have had great success with both systems.

You must, must, must practice with these bow-mounted decoys before taking them afield. Both give the bow a different feel. The first time I used my Heads-Up Strutting Turkey in the field, I missed three different birds.

As you're practicing with your bow-mounted decoy, I also highly recommend you test it out in windy conditions. The windier it is, the harder it is to be accurate with a bow-mounted decoy. The large cloth surface area acts like a sail.

What I've discovered about running and gunning with a bow-mounted decoy is two-fold. First, when it works, there is not a more thrilling way to bowhunt wild birds. Second, when it doesn't, you end up covering lots of miles on foot. That's all well and good, but it means you end up spooking lots of birds.

As for as the time of year these bow-mounted fakes work best, I've had great success from the beginning of the season to the end. I've discovered it's all about the temperature of the tom or toms I'm trying to dupe. I've had success glassing up one or more toms guarding hens and then moving in on them. Typically, if you can get within 100 yards before showing the bird the decoy, you should have some quick action. Another high-success situation is slipping in on a lone tom that is covering lots of ground and gobbling as he goes. A wandering, gobbling tom is looking for love, and I've had these birds come running at full tilt. More than once I've shot a bird behind a bow-mounted decoy at less than 5 yards. It will get your blood pumping.

Another made-in-Heaven bow-mounted opportunity is when you can glass a bird's spurs from a distance. Dominant three-, four- and five-year-old birds often won't tolerate an intruder. If your goal is to kill an older bird, a bow-mounted hunt can yield great results.

I realize many reading this book may have no interest in jakes. I'm not sure why, but I'm all about each hunter doing whatever makes him or her happy. Jakes make me very happy, and if a stubby beard gives you an ear-to-ear grin as well, don't be afraid to show a single or even a gaggle of jakes your bow-mounted tom. It's not uncommon for a group of jakes to gang up on a lone tom. More than once I've brought multiple jakes bowhunting-close with my bow-mounted tom decoys. I've also had a few curious lone jakes come in as well, though both hung up at 30 yards, forcing me to take a longer shot.

My favorite run-and-gun technique is the buddy system. Both decoys work well for this, and what I love about this style of bowhunting birds is the camaraderie and the fact that I don't have to have anything extra mounted to my bow. Plus, the decoyer can be a little bit more mobile, and the shooter can hang back in the cover if need be. The key to the buddy system is communication and safety. I have zero problems crawling out in front of a trusted buddy and having him behind me with his bow. I know my buddy will only take the shot if there is absolutely no danger to me. If the decoyer crawls out in front, always make sure to position yourself to one side or another. You never want the decoyer directly in front of you. Again, communication and trust is the key to this type of decoying. Never take a shot that feels even remotely dangerous.

NOTE: When using a bow-mounted decoy, don't be afraid to move on birds even when they're looking at you. If a bird hangs up, I will always twist and turn my bow, moving the fan one way and then another. Sometimes this movement is all it takes to get a bird to resume his approach. If this doesn't work, I start crawling toward the bird. Twice I've been able to simply crawl bowhunting-close and get shots at uninterested toms.

NOTE: You can't overlook safety when using a bow-mounted decoy. Remember, you are the decoy, and the only thing separating you from a load of lead or a broadhead-tipped arrow is cloth. There are a lot of over-eager hunters out there, and these decoys do look very realistic. Typically, I don't use a bow-mounted decoy if I'm hunting public land, and if shotgun season is open, typically becomes never. It's just not worth it. If I'm hunting public land during the archery-only season, I will use a bow-mounted decoy from time to time. I always feel better about the situation if my truck is the only one in the parking lot, or if I have a chance to visit with other the hunters sharing the area with me. If I get this chance to exchange pleasantries, I always take it, and I let them know my bowhunting plans. When it comes to private land, I use my bow-mounted decoys a lot more. Most of the time I have exclusive rights to the land. Even when I don't, I'm typically in contact with the other hunters that are sharing the property with me.

THAT'S IT! You're done! Remember, the tips, tactics and gear mentioned in this piece came from the school of hard knocks. Put them into practice, and I truly believe you will experience your most enjoyable and successful spring to date.

Made in the USA
Middletown, DE
19 February 2020